This book belongs to:

. . . .

. . . .

. . . .

Free Goodies! Visit Our Website : PodTreasury.com

Today Is:______________________

MORNING

- ☐ Make Your Bed
- ☐ Get Dressed
- ☐ Eat Breakfast
- ☐ Brush Teeth
- ☐ Brush Hair
- ☐ Get Backpack Ready
- ☐ Put Shoes On

BEDTIME

- ☐ Clean Room
- ☐ Bath Time
- ☐ Put On Pajamas
- ☐ Brush Teeth
- ☐ Potty Time
- ☐ Read Book
- ☐ Goodnight Kiss

MORNING

- ☐ Make Your Bed
- ☐ Get Dressed
- ☐ Eat Breakfast
- ☐ Brush Teeth
- ☐ Brush Hair
- ☐ Get Backpack Ready
- ☐ Put Shoes On

BEDTIME

- ☐ Clean Room
- ☐ Bath Time
- ☐ Put On Pajamas
- ☐ Brush Teeth
- ☐ Potty Time
- ☐ Read Book
- ☐ Goodnight Kiss

Today Is:________________

MORNING

- ☐ Make Your Bed
- ☐ Get Dressed
- ☐ Eat Breakfast
- ☐ Brush Teeth
- ☐ Brush Hair
- ☐ Get Backpack Ready
- ☐ Put Shoes On

BEDTIME

- ☐ Clean Room
- ☐ Bath Time
- ☐ Put On Pajamas
- ☐ Brush Teeth
- ☐ Potty Time
- ☐ Read Book
- ☐ Goodnight Kiss

Today Is:_______________________

MORNING

- [ ] Make Your Bed
- [ ] Get Dressed
- [ ] Eat Breakfast
- [ ] Brush Teeth
- [ ] Brush Hair
- [ ] Get Backpack Ready
- [ ] Put Shoes On

BEDTIME

- [ ] Clean Room
- [ ] Bath Time
- [ ] Put On Pajamas
- [ ] Brush Teeth
- [ ] Potty Time
- [ ] Read Book
- [ ] Goodnight Kiss

Today Is:______________

MORNING

- ☐ Make Your Bed
- ☐ Get Dressed
- ☐ Eat Breakfast
- ☐ Brush Teeth
- ☐ Brush Hair
- ☐ Get Backpack Ready
- ☐ Put Shoes On

BEDTIME

- ☐ Clean Room
- ☐ Bath Time
- ☐ Put On Pajamas
- ☐ Brush Teeth
- ☐ Potty Time
- ☐ Read Book
- ☐ Goodnight Kiss

MORNING

- [ ] Make Your Bed
- [ ] Get Dressed
- [ ] Eat Breakfast
- [ ] Brush Teeth
- [ ] Brush Hair
- [ ] Get Backpack Ready
- [ ] Put Shoes On

BEDTIME

- [ ] Clean Room
- [ ] Bath Time
- [ ] Put On Pajamas
- [ ] Brush Teeth
- [ ] Potty Time
- [ ] Read Book
- [ ] Goodnight Kiss

MORNING

- ☐ Make Your Bed
- ☐ Get Dressed
- ☐ Eat Breakfast
- ☐ Brush Teeth
- ☐ Brush Hair
- ☐ Get Backpack Ready
- ☐ Put Shoes On

BEDTIME

- ☐ Clean Room
- ☐ Bath Time
- ☐ Put On Pajamas
- ☐ Brush Teeth
- ☐ Potty Time
- ☐ Read Book
- ☐ Goodnight Kiss

MORNING

- ☐ Make Your Bed
- ☐ Get Dressed
- ☐ Eat Breakfast
- ☐ Brush Teeth
- ☐ Brush Hair
- ☐ Get Backpack Ready
- ☐ Put Shoes On

BEDTIME

- ☐ Clean Room
- ☐ Bath Time
- ☐ Put On Pajamas
- ☐ Brush Teeth
- ☐ Potty Time
- ☐ Read Book
- ☐ Goodnight Kiss

Today Is:________

MORNING

- ☐ Make Your Bed
- ☐ Get Dressed
- ☐ Eat Breakfast
- ☐ Brush Teeth
- ☐ Brush Hair
- ☐ Get Backpack Ready
- ☐ Put Shoes On

BEDTIME

- ☐ Clean Room
- ☐ Bath Time
- ☐ Put On Pajamas
- ☐ Brush Teeth
- ☐ Potty Time
- ☐ Read Book
- ☐ Goodnight Kiss

MORNING

- ☐ Make Your Bed
- ☐ Get Dressed
- ☐ Eat Breakfast
- ☐ Brush Teeth
- ☐ Brush Hair
- ☐ Get Backpack Ready
- ☐ Put Shoes On

BEDTIME

- ☐ Clean Room
- ☐ Bath Time
- ☐ Put On Pajamas
- ☐ Brush Teeth
- ☐ Potty Time
- ☐ Read Book
- ☐ Goodnight Kiss

Today Is:_______________

MORNING

- ☐ Make Your Bed
- ☐ Get Dressed
- ☐ Eat Breakfast
- ☐ Brush Teeth
- ☐ Brush Hair
- ☐ Get Backpack Ready
- ☐ Put Shoes On

BEDTIME

- ☐ Clean Room
- ☐ Bath Time
- ☐ Put On Pajamas
- ☐ Brush Teeth
- ☐ Potty Time
- ☐ Read Book
- ☐ Goodnight Kiss

MORNING

- ☐ Make Your Bed
- ☐ Get Dressed
- ☐ Eat Breakfast
- ☐ Brush Teeth
- ☐ Brush Hair
- ☐ Get Backpack Ready
- ☐ Put Shoes On

BEDTIME

- ☐ Clean Room
- ☐ Bath Time
- ☐ Put On Pajamas
- ☐ Brush Teeth
- ☐ Potty Time
- ☐ Read Book
- ☐ Goodnight Kiss

MORNING

- ☐ Make Your Bed
- ☐ Get Dressed
- ☐ Eat Breakfast
- ☐ Brush Teeth
- ☐ Brush Hair
- ☐ Get Backpack Ready
- ☐ Put Shoes On

BEDTIME

- ☐ Clean Room
- ☐ Bath Time
- ☐ Put On Pajamas
- ☐ Brush Teeth
- ☐ Potty Time
- ☐ Read Book
- ☐ Goodnight Kiss

Today Is:＿＿＿＿＿＿＿＿＿＿

MORNING

- ☐ Make Your Bed
- ☐ Get Dressed
- ☐ Eat Breakfast
- ☐ Brush Teeth
- ☐ Brush Hair
- ☐ Get Backpack Ready
- ☐ Put Shoes On

BEDTIME

- ☐ Clean Room
- ☐ Bath Time
- ☐ Put On Pajamas
- ☐ Brush Teeth
- ☐ Potty Time
- ☐ Read Book
- ☐ Goodnight Kiss

Today Is:_______________

MORNING

- ☐ Make Your Bed
- ☐ Get Dressed
- ☐ Eat Breakfast
- ☐ Brush Teeth
- ☐ Brush Hair
- ☐ Get Backpack Ready
- ☐ Put Shoes On

BEDTIME

- ☐ Clean Room
- ☐ Bath Time
- ☐ Put On Pajamas
- ☐ Brush Teeth
- ☐ Potty Time
- ☐ Read Book
- ☐ Goodnight Kiss

MORNING

- ☐ Make Your Bed
- ☐ Get Dressed
- ☐ Eat Breakfast
- ☐ Brush Teeth
- ☐ Brush Hair
- ☐ Get Backpack Ready
- ☐ Put Shoes On

BEDTIME

- ☐ Clean Room
- ☐ Bath Time
- ☐ Put On Pajamas
- ☐ Brush Teeth
- ☐ Potty Time
- ☐ Read Book
- ☐ Goodnight Kiss

Today Is:____________

MORNING

- ☐ Make Your Bed
- ☐ Get Dressed
- ☐ Eat Breakfast
- ☐ Brush Teeth
- ☐ Brush Hair
- ☐ Get Backpack Ready
- ☐ Put Shoes On

BEDTIME

- ☐ Clean Room
- ☐ Bath Time
- ☐ Put On Pajamas
- ☐ Brush Teeth
- ☐ Potty Time
- ☐ Read Book
- ☐ Goodnight Kiss

Today Is:_______________________________

MORNING

- [ ] Make Your Bed
- [ ] Get Dressed
- [ ] Eat Breakfast
- [ ] Brush Teeth
- [ ] Brush Hair
- [ ] Get Backpack Ready
- [ ] Put Shoes On

BEDTIME

- [ ] Clean Room
- [ ] Bath Time
- [ ] Put On Pajamas
- [ ] Brush Teeth
- [ ] Potty Time
- [ ] Read Book
- [ ] Goodnight Kiss

MORNING

- ☐ Make Your Bed
- ☐ Get Dressed
- ☐ Eat Breakfast
- ☐ Brush Teeth
- ☐ Brush Hair
- ☐ Get Backpack Ready
- ☐ Put Shoes On

BEDTIME

- ☐ Clean Room
- ☐ Bath Time
- ☐ Put On Pajamas
- ☐ Brush Teeth
- ☐ Potty Time
- ☐ Read Book
- ☐ Goodnight Kiss

MORNING

- ☐ Make Your Bed
- ☐ Get Dressed
- ☐ Eat Breakfast
- ☐ Brush Teeth
- ☐ Brush Hair
- ☐ Get Backpack Ready
- ☐ Put Shoes On

BEDTIME

- ☐ Clean Room
- ☐ Bath Time
- ☐ Put On Pajamas
- ☐ Brush Teeth
- ☐ Potty Time
- ☐ Read Book
- ☐ Goodnight Kiss

Today Is:________________

MORNING

- ☐ Make Your Bed
- ☐ Get Dressed
- ☐ Eat Breakfast
- ☐ Brush Teeth
- ☐ Brush Hair
- ☐ Get Backpack Ready
- ☐ Put Shoes On

BEDTIME

- ☐ Clean Room
- ☐ Bath Time
- ☐ Put On Pajamas
- ☐ Brush Teeth
- ☐ Potty Time
- ☐ Read Book
- ☐ Goodnight Kiss

MORNING

- ☐ Make Your Bed
- ☐ Get Dressed
- ☐ Eat Breakfast
- ☐ Brush Teeth
- ☐ Brush Hair
- ☐ Get Backpack Ready
- ☐ Put Shoes On

BEDTIME

- ☐ Clean Room
- ☐ Bath Time
- ☐ Put On Pajamas
- ☐ Brush Teeth
- ☐ Potty Time
- ☐ Read Book
- ☐ Goodnight Kiss

Today Is:_____________

MORNING

- ☐ Make Your Bed
- ☐ Get Dressed
- ☐ Eat Breakfast
- ☐ Brush Teeth
- ☐ Brush Hair
- ☐ Get Backpack Ready
- ☐ Put Shoes On

BEDTIME

- ☐ Clean Room
- ☐ Bath Time
- ☐ Put On Pajamas
- ☐ Brush Teeth
- ☐ Potty Time
- ☐ Read Book
- ☐ Goodnight Kiss

Today Is:_______________

MORNING

- ☐ Make Your Bed
- ☐ Get Dressed
- ☐ Eat Breakfast
- ☐ Brush Teeth
- ☐ Brush Hair
- ☐ Get Backpack Ready
- ☐ Put Shoes On

BEDTIME

- ☐ Clean Room
- ☐ Bath Time
- ☐ Put On Pajamas
- ☐ Brush Teeth
- ☐ Potty Time
- ☐ Read Book
- ☐ Goodnight Kiss

Today Is:_______________

MORNING

- ☐ Make Your Bed
- ☐ Get Dressed
- ☐ Eat Breakfast
- ☐ Brush Teeth
- ☐ Brush Hair
- ☐ Get Backpack Ready
- ☐ Put Shoes On

BEDTIME

- ☐ Clean Room
- ☐ Bath Time
- ☐ Put On Pajamas
- ☐ Brush Teeth
- ☐ Potty Time
- ☐ Read Book
- ☐ Goodnight Kiss

Today Is:______________

<table>
<tr><td>

MORNING

- ☐ Make Your Bed
- ☐ Get Dressed
- ☐ Eat Breakfast
- ☐ Brush Teeth
- ☐ Brush Hair
- ☐ Get Backpack Ready
- ☐ Put Shoes On

</td><td>

BEDTIME

- ☐ Clean Room
- ☐ Bath Time
- ☐ Put On Pajamas
- ☐ Brush Teeth
- ☐ Potty Time
- ☐ Read Book
- ☐ Goodnight Kiss

</td></tr>
</table>

Today Is:________________

MORNING

- ☐ Make Your Bed
- ☐ Get Dressed
- ☐ Eat Breakfast
- ☐ Brush Teeth
- ☐ Brush Hair
- ☐ Get Backpack Ready
- ☐ Put Shoes On

BEDTIME

- ☐ Clean Room
- ☐ Bath Time
- ☐ Put On Pajamas
- ☐ Brush Teeth
- ☐ Potty Time
- ☐ Read Book
- ☐ Goodnight Kiss

MORNING

- ☐ Make Your Bed
- ☐ Get Dressed
- ☐ Eat Breakfast
- ☐ Brush Teeth
- ☐ Brush Hair
- ☐ Get Backpack Ready
- ☐ Put Shoes On

BEDTIME

- ☐ Clean Room
- ☐ Bath Time
- ☐ Put On Pajamas
- ☐ Brush Teeth
- ☐ Potty Time
- ☐ Read Book
- ☐ Goodnight Kiss

MORNING

- ☐ Make Your Bed
- ☐ Get Dressed
- ☐ Eat Breakfast
- ☐ Brush Teeth
- ☐ Brush Hair
- ☐ Get Backpack Ready
- ☐ Put Shoes On

BEDTIME

- ☐ Clean Room
- ☐ Bath Time
- ☐ Put On Pajamas
- ☐ Brush Teeth
- ☐ Potty Time
- ☐ Read Book
- ☐ Goodnight Kiss

Today Is:_______________________

MORNING

- ☐ Make Your Bed
- ☐ Get Dressed
- ☐ Eat Breakfast
- ☐ Brush Teeth
- ☐ Brush Hair
- ☐ Get Backpack Ready
- ☐ Put Shoes On

BEDTIME

- ☐ Clean Room
- ☐ Bath Time
- ☐ Put On Pajamas
- ☐ Brush Teeth
- ☐ Potty Time
- ☐ Read Book
- ☐ Goodnight Kiss

Today Is:________________________

<table>
<tr><td>

MORNING

☐ Make Your Bed

☐ Get Dressed

☐ Eat Breakfast

☐ Brush Teeth

☐ Brush Hair

☐ Get Backpack Ready

☐ Put Shoes On

</td><td>

BEDTIME

☐ Clean Room

☐ Bath Time

☐ Put On Pajamas

☐ Brush Teeth

☐ Potty Time

☐ Read Book

☐ Goodnight Kiss

</td></tr>
</table>

MORNING

- ☐ Make Your Bed
- ☐ Get Dressed
- ☐ Eat Breakfast
- ☐ Brush Teeth
- ☐ Brush Hair
- ☐ Get Backpack Ready
- ☐ Put Shoes On

BEDTIME

- ☐ Clean Room
- ☐ Bath Time
- ☐ Put On Pajamas
- ☐ Brush Teeth
- ☐ Potty Time
- ☐ Read Book
- ☐ Goodnight Kiss

Today Is:_______________

MORNING

- ☐ Make Your Bed
- ☐ Get Dressed
- ☐ Eat Breakfast
- ☐ Brush Teeth
- ☐ Brush Hair
- ☐ Get Backpack Ready
- ☐ Put Shoes On

BEDTIME

- ☐ Clean Room
- ☐ Bath Time
- ☐ Put On Pajamas
- ☐ Brush Teeth
- ☐ Potty Time
- ☐ Read Book
- ☐ Goodnight Kiss

Today Is:_________________

MORNING

- ☐ Make Your Bed
- ☐ Get Dressed
- ☐ Eat Breakfast
- ☐ Brush Teeth
- ☐ Brush Hair
- ☐ Get Backpack Ready
- ☐ Put Shoes On

BEDTIME

- ☐ Clean Room
- ☐ Bath Time
- ☐ Put On Pajamas
- ☐ Brush Teeth
- ☐ Potty Time
- ☐ Read Book
- ☐ Goodnight Kiss

Today Is:________________

MORNING

- ☐ Make Your Bed
- ☐ Get Dressed
- ☐ Eat Breakfast
- ☐ Brush Teeth
- ☐ Brush Hair
- ☐ Get Backpack Ready
- ☐ Put Shoes On

BEDTIME

- ☐ Clean Room
- ☐ Bath Time
- ☐ Put On Pajamas
- ☐ Brush Teeth
- ☐ Potty Time
- ☐ Read Book
- ☐ Goodnight Kiss

Today Is:_______________

MORNING

- ☐ Make Your Bed
- ☐ Get Dressed
- ☐ Eat Breakfast
- ☐ Brush Teeth
- ☐ Brush Hair
- ☐ Get Backpack Ready
- ☐ Put Shoes On

BEDTIME

- ☐ Clean Room
- ☐ Bath Time
- ☐ Put On Pajamas
- ☐ Brush Teeth
- ☐ Potty Time
- ☐ Read Book
- ☐ Goodnight Kiss

Today Is:_____________________

MORNING

- ☐ Make Your Bed
- ☐ Get Dressed
- ☐ Eat Breakfast
- ☐ Brush Teeth
- ☐ Brush Hair
- ☐ Get Backpack Ready
- ☐ Put Shoes On

BEDTIME

- ☐ Clean Room
- ☐ Bath Time
- ☐ Put On Pajamas
- ☐ Brush Teeth
- ☐ Potty Time
- ☐ Read Book
- ☐ Goodnight Kiss

Today Is:______________________

MORNING

- [ ] Make Your Bed
- [ ] Get Dressed
- [ ] Eat Breakfast
- [ ] Brush Teeth
- [ ] Brush Hair
- [ ] Get Backpack Ready
- [ ] Put Shoes On

BEDTIME

- [ ] Clean Room
- [ ] Bath Time
- [ ] Put On Pajamas
- [ ] Brush Teeth
- [ ] Potty Time
- [ ] Read Book
- [ ] Goodnight Kiss

MORNING

- ☐ Make Your Bed
- ☐ Get Dressed
- ☐ Eat Breakfast
- ☐ Brush Teeth
- ☐ Brush Hair
- ☐ Get Backpack Ready
- ☐ Put Shoes On

BEDTIME

- ☐ Clean Room
- ☐ Bath Time
- ☐ Put On Pajamas
- ☐ Brush Teeth
- ☐ Potty Time
- ☐ Read Book
- ☐ Goodnight Kiss

MORNING

- ☐ Make Your Bed
- ☐ Get Dressed
- ☐ Eat Breakfast
- ☐ Brush Teeth
- ☐ Brush Hair
- ☐ Get Backpack Ready
- ☐ Put Shoes On

BEDTIME

- ☐ Clean Room
- ☐ Bath Time
- ☐ Put On Pajamas
- ☐ Brush Teeth
- ☐ Potty Time
- ☐ Read Book
- ☐ Goodnight Kiss

Today Is:____________________

MORNING

- ☐ Make Your Bed
- ☐ Get Dressed
- ☐ Eat Breakfast
- ☐ Brush Teeth
- ☐ Brush Hair
- ☐ Get Backpack Ready
- ☐ Put Shoes On

BEDTIME

- ☐ Clean Room
- ☐ Bath Time
- ☐ Put On Pajamas
- ☐ Brush Teeth
- ☐ Potty Time
- ☐ Read Book
- ☐ Goodnight Kiss

Today Is:________________

MORNING

- ☐ Make Your Bed
- ☐ Get Dressed
- ☐ Eat Breakfast
- ☐ Brush Teeth
- ☐ Brush Hair
- ☐ Get Backpack Ready
- ☐ Put Shoes On

BEDTIME

- ☐ Clean Room
- ☐ Bath Time
- ☐ Put On Pajamas
- ☐ Brush Teeth
- ☐ Potty Time
- ☐ Read Book
- ☐ Goodnight Kiss

Today Is:_______________

MORNING

- [ ] Make Your Bed
- [ ] Get Dressed
- [ ] Eat Breakfast
- [ ] Brush Teeth
- [ ] Brush Hair
- [ ] Get Backpack Ready
- [ ] Put Shoes On

BEDTIME

- [ ] Clean Room
- [ ] Bath Time
- [ ] Put On Pajamas
- [ ] Brush Teeth
- [ ] Potty Time
- [ ] Read Book
- [ ] Goodnight Kiss

Today Is:________________

MORNING

- [ ] Make Your Bed
- [ ] Get Dressed
- [ ] Eat Breakfast
- [ ] Brush Teeth
- [ ] Brush Hair
- [ ] Get Backpack Ready
- [ ] Put Shoes On

BEDTIME

- [ ] Clean Room
- [ ] Bath Time
- [ ] Put On Pajamas
- [ ] Brush Teeth
- [ ] Potty Time
- [ ] Read Book
- [ ] Goodnight Kiss

Today Is:________________

MORNING

- [ ] Make Your Bed
- [ ] Get Dressed
- [ ] Eat Breakfast
- [ ] Brush Teeth
- [ ] Brush Hair
- [ ] Get Backpack Ready
- [ ] Put Shoes On

BEDTIME

- [ ] Clean Room
- [ ] Bath Time
- [ ] Put On Pajamas
- [ ] Brush Teeth
- [ ] Potty Time
- [ ] Read Book
- [ ] Goodnight Kiss

MORNING

- ☐ Make Your Bed
- ☐ Get Dressed
- ☐ Eat Breakfast
- ☐ Brush Teeth
- ☐ Brush Hair
- ☐ Get Backpack Ready
- ☐ Put Shoes On

BEDTIME

- ☐ Clean Room
- ☐ Bath Time
- ☐ Put On Pajamas
- ☐ Brush Teeth
- ☐ Potty Time
- ☐ Read Book
- ☐ Goodnight Kiss

MORNING

- ☐ Make Your Bed
- ☐ Get Dressed
- ☐ Eat Breakfast
- ☐ Brush Teeth
- ☐ Brush Hair
- ☐ Get Backpack Ready
- ☐ Put Shoes On

BEDTIME

- ☐ Clean Room
- ☐ Bath Time
- ☐ Put On Pajamas
- ☐ Brush Teeth
- ☐ Potty Time
- ☐ Read Book
- ☐ Goodnight Kiss

MORNING

- ☐ Make Your Bed
- ☐ Get Dressed
- ☐ Eat Breakfast
- ☐ Brush Teeth
- ☐ Brush Hair
- ☐ Get Backpack Ready
- ☐ Put Shoes On

BEDTIME

- ☐ Clean Room
- ☐ Bath Time
- ☐ Put On Pajamas
- ☐ Brush Teeth
- ☐ Potty Time
- ☐ Read Book
- ☐ Goodnight Kiss

MORNING

- ☐ Make Your Bed
- ☐ Get Dressed
- ☐ Eat Breakfast
- ☐ Brush Teeth
- ☐ Brush Hair
- ☐ Get Backpack Ready
- ☐ Put Shoes On

BEDTIME

- ☐ Clean Room
- ☐ Bath Time
- ☐ Put On Pajamas
- ☐ Brush Teeth
- ☐ Potty Time
- ☐ Read Book
- ☐ Goodnight Kiss

MORNING

- ☐ Make Your Bed
- ☐ Get Dressed
- ☐ Eat Breakfast
- ☐ Brush Teeth
- ☐ Brush Hair
- ☐ Get Backpack Ready
- ☐ Put Shoes On

BEDTIME

- ☐ Clean Room
- ☐ Bath Time
- ☐ Put On Pajamas
- ☐ Brush Teeth
- ☐ Potty Time
- ☐ Read Book
- ☐ Goodnight Kiss

Today Is:___________________

<table>
<tr><td>

MORNING

☐ Make Your Bed

☐ Get Dressed

☐ Eat Breakfast

☐ Brush Teeth

☐ Brush Hair

☐ Get Backpack Ready

☐ Put Shoes On

</td><td>

BEDTIME

☐ Clean Room

☐ Bath Time

☐ Put On Pajamas

☐ Brush Teeth

☐ Potty Time

☐ Read Book

☐ Goodnight Kiss

</td></tr>
</table>

MORNING

- ☐ Make Your Bed
- ☐ Get Dressed
- ☐ Eat Breakfast
- ☐ Brush Teeth
- ☐ Brush Hair
- ☐ Get Backpack Ready
- ☐ Put Shoes On

BEDTIME

- ☐ Clean Room
- ☐ Bath Time
- ☐ Put On Pajamas
- ☐ Brush Teeth
- ☐ Potty Time
- ☐ Read Book
- ☐ Goodnight Kiss

MORNING

- ☐ Make Your Bed
- ☐ Get Dressed
- ☐ Eat Breakfast
- ☐ Brush Teeth
- ☐ Brush Hair
- ☐ Get Backpack Ready
- ☐ Put Shoes On

BEDTIME

- ☐ Clean Room
- ☐ Bath Time
- ☐ Put On Pajamas
- ☐ Brush Teeth
- ☐ Potty Time
- ☐ Read Book
- ☐ Goodnight Kiss

MORNING

- ☐ Make Your Bed
- ☐ Get Dressed
- ☐ Eat Breakfast
- ☐ Brush Teeth
- ☐ Brush Hair
- ☐ Get Backpack Ready
- ☐ Put Shoes On

BEDTIME

- ☐ Clean Room
- ☐ Bath Time
- ☐ Put On Pajamas
- ☐ Brush Teeth
- ☐ Potty Time
- ☐ Read Book
- ☐ Goodnight Kiss

Today Is:________________

MORNING

- ☐ Make Your Bed
- ☐ Get Dressed
- ☐ Eat Breakfast
- ☐ Brush Teeth
- ☐ Brush Hair
- ☐ Get Backpack Ready
- ☐ Put Shoes On

BEDTIME

- ☐ Clean Room
- ☐ Bath Time
- ☐ Put On Pajamas
- ☐ Brush Teeth
- ☐ Potty Time
- ☐ Read Book
- ☐ Goodnight Kiss

Today Is:_______________

MORNING

- ☐ Make Your Bed
- ☐ Get Dressed
- ☐ Eat Breakfast
- ☐ Brush Teeth
- ☐ Brush Hair
- ☐ Get Backpack Ready
- ☐ Put Shoes On

BEDTIME

- ☐ Clean Room
- ☐ Bath Time
- ☐ Put On Pajamas
- ☐ Brush Teeth
- ☐ Potty Time
- ☐ Read Book
- ☐ Goodnight Kiss

MORNING

- ☐ Make Your Bed
- ☐ Get Dressed
- ☐ Eat Breakfast
- ☐ Brush Teeth
- ☐ Brush Hair
- ☐ Get Backpack Ready
- ☐ Put Shoes On

BEDTIME

- ☐ Clean Room
- ☐ Bath Time
- ☐ Put On Pajamas
- ☐ Brush Teeth
- ☐ Potty Time
- ☐ Read Book
- ☐ Goodnight Kiss

MORNING

- ☐ Make Your Bed
- ☐ Get Dressed
- ☐ Eat Breakfast
- ☐ Brush Teeth
- ☐ Brush Hair
- ☐ Get Backpack Ready
- ☐ Put Shoes On

BEDTIME

- ☐ Clean Room
- ☐ Bath Time
- ☐ Put On Pajamas
- ☐ Brush Teeth
- ☐ Potty Time
- ☐ Read Book
- ☐ Goodnight Kiss

Today Is:_______________

MORNING

- ☐ Make Your Bed
- ☐ Get Dressed
- ☐ Eat Breakfast
- ☐ Brush Teeth
- ☐ Brush Hair
- ☐ Get Backpack Ready
- ☐ Put Shoes On

BEDTIME

- ☐ Clean Room
- ☐ Bath Time
- ☐ Put On Pajamas
- ☐ Brush Teeth
- ☐ Potty Time
- ☐ Read Book
- ☐ Goodnight Kiss

Today Is:_______________

MORNING

- ☐ Make Your Bed
- ☐ Get Dressed
- ☐ Eat Breakfast
- ☐ Brush Teeth
- ☐ Brush Hair
- ☐ Get Backpack Ready
- ☐ Put Shoes On

BEDTIME

- ☐ Clean Room
- ☐ Bath Time
- ☐ Put On Pajamas
- ☐ Brush Teeth
- ☐ Potty Time
- ☐ Read Book
- ☐ Goodnight Kiss

Today Is:______________

MORNING

- ☐ Make Your Bed
- ☐ Get Dressed
- ☐ Eat Breakfast
- ☐ Brush Teeth
- ☐ Brush Hair
- ☐ Get Backpack Ready
- ☐ Put Shoes On

BEDTIME

- ☐ Clean Room
- ☐ Bath Time
- ☐ Put On Pajamas
- ☐ Brush Teeth
- ☐ Potty Time
- ☐ Read Book
- ☐ Goodnight Kiss

Today Is:_______________________

MORNING

- ☐ Make Your Bed
- ☐ Get Dressed
- ☐ Eat Breakfast
- ☐ Brush Teeth
- ☐ Brush Hair
- ☐ Get Backpack Ready
- ☐ Put Shoes On

BEDTIME

- ☐ Clean Room
- ☐ Bath Time
- ☐ Put On Pajamas
- ☐ Brush Teeth
- ☐ Potty Time
- ☐ Read Book
- ☐ Goodnight Kiss

Today Is:________________

MORNING

- ☐ Make Your Bed
- ☐ Get Dressed
- ☐ Eat Breakfast
- ☐ Brush Teeth
- ☐ Brush Hair
- ☐ Get Backpack Ready
- ☐ Put Shoes On

BEDTIME

- ☐ Clean Room
- ☐ Bath Time
- ☐ Put On Pajamas
- ☐ Brush Teeth
- ☐ Potty Time
- ☐ Read Book
- ☐ Goodnight Kiss

Today Is:________________

MORNING

- [ ] Make Your Bed
- [ ] Get Dressed
- [ ] Eat Breakfast
- [ ] Brush Teeth
- [ ] Brush Hair
- [ ] Get Backpack Ready
- [ ] Put Shoes On

BEDTIME

- [ ] Clean Room
- [ ] Bath Time
- [ ] Put On Pajamas
- [ ] Brush Teeth
- [ ] Potty Time
- [ ] Read Book
- [ ] Goodnight Kiss

Today Is:________________

MORNING

- ☐ Make Your Bed
- ☐ Get Dressed
- ☐ Eat Breakfast
- ☐ Brush Teeth
- ☐ Brush Hair
- ☐ Get Backpack Ready
- ☐ Put Shoes On

BEDTIME

- ☐ Clean Room
- ☐ Bath Time
- ☐ Put On Pajamas
- ☐ Brush Teeth
- ☐ Potty Time
- ☐ Read Book
- ☐ Goodnight Kiss

MORNING

- ☐ Make Your Bed
- ☐ Get Dressed
- ☐ Eat Breakfast
- ☐ Brush Teeth
- ☐ Brush Hair
- ☐ Get Backpack Ready
- ☐ Put Shoes On

BEDTIME

- ☐ Clean Room
- ☐ Bath Time
- ☐ Put On Pajamas
- ☐ Brush Teeth
- ☐ Potty Time
- ☐ Read Book
- ☐ Goodnight Kiss

MORNING

- ☐ Make Your Bed
- ☐ Get Dressed
- ☐ Eat Breakfast
- ☐ Brush Teeth
- ☐ Brush Hair
- ☐ Get Backpack Ready
- ☐ Put Shoes On

BEDTIME

- ☐ Clean Room
- ☐ Bath Time
- ☐ Put On Pajamas
- ☐ Brush Teeth
- ☐ Potty Time
- ☐ Read Book
- ☐ Goodnight Kiss

MORNING

- ☐ Make Your Bed
- ☐ Get Dressed
- ☐ Eat Breakfast
- ☐ Brush Teeth
- ☐ Brush Hair
- ☐ Get Backpack Ready
- ☐ Put Shoes On

BEDTIME

- ☐ Clean Room
- ☐ Bath Time
- ☐ Put On Pajamas
- ☐ Brush Teeth
- ☐ Potty Time
- ☐ Read Book
- ☐ Goodnight Kiss

MORNING

- ☐ Make Your Bed
- ☐ Get Dressed
- ☐ Eat Breakfast
- ☐ Brush Teeth
- ☐ Brush Hair
- ☐ Get Backpack Ready
- ☐ Put Shoes On

BEDTIME

- ☐ Clean Room
- ☐ Bath Time
- ☐ Put On Pajamas
- ☐ Brush Teeth
- ☐ Potty Time
- ☐ Read Book
- ☐ Goodnight Kiss

Today Is:_______________

MORNING

- ☐ Make Your Bed
- ☐ Get Dressed
- ☐ Eat Breakfast
- ☐ Brush Teeth
- ☐ Brush Hair
- ☐ Get Backpack Ready
- ☐ Put Shoes On

BEDTIME

- ☐ Clean Room
- ☐ Bath Time
- ☐ Put On Pajamas
- ☐ Brush Teeth
- ☐ Potty Time
- ☐ Read Book
- ☐ Goodnight Kiss

MORNING

- ☐ Make Your Bed
- ☐ Get Dressed
- ☐ Eat Breakfast
- ☐ Brush Teeth
- ☐ Brush Hair
- ☐ Get Backpack Ready
- ☐ Put Shoes On

BEDTIME

- ☐ Clean Room
- ☐ Bath Time
- ☐ Put On Pajamas
- ☐ Brush Teeth
- ☐ Potty Time
- ☐ Read Book
- ☐ Goodnight Kiss

Today Is:________________

MORNING

- ☐ Make Your Bed
- ☐ Get Dressed
- ☐ Eat Breakfast
- ☐ Brush Teeth
- ☐ Brush Hair
- ☐ Get Backpack Ready
- ☐ Put Shoes On

BEDTIME

- ☐ Clean Room
- ☐ Bath Time
- ☐ Put On Pajamas
- ☐ Brush Teeth
- ☐ Potty Time
- ☐ Read Book
- ☐ Goodnight Kiss

MORNING

- ☐ Make Your Bed
- ☐ Get Dressed
- ☐ Eat Breakfast
- ☐ Brush Teeth
- ☐ Brush Hair
- ☐ Get Backpack Ready
- ☐ Put Shoes On

BEDTIME

- ☐ Clean Room
- ☐ Bath Time
- ☐ Put On Pajamas
- ☐ Brush Teeth
- ☐ Potty Time
- ☐ Read Book
- ☐ Goodnight Kiss

MORNING

- ☐ Make Your Bed
- ☐ Get Dressed
- ☐ Eat Breakfast
- ☐ Brush Teeth
- ☐ Brush Hair
- ☐ Get Backpack Ready
- ☐ Put Shoes On

BEDTIME

- ☐ Clean Room
- ☐ Bath Time
- ☐ Put On Pajamas
- ☐ Brush Teeth
- ☐ Potty Time
- ☐ Read Book
- ☐ Goodnight Kiss

Today Is:_______________

MORNING

- ☐ Make Your Bed
- ☐ Get Dressed
- ☐ Eat Breakfast
- ☐ Brush Teeth
- ☐ Brush Hair
- ☐ Get Backpack Ready
- ☐ Put Shoes On

BEDTIME

- ☐ Clean Room
- ☐ Bath Time
- ☐ Put On Pajamas
- ☐ Brush Teeth
- ☐ Potty Time
- ☐ Read Book
- ☐ Goodnight Kiss

Today Is:________________

MORNING

- ☐ Make Your Bed
- ☐ Get Dressed
- ☐ Eat Breakfast
- ☐ Brush Teeth
- ☐ Brush Hair
- ☐ Get Backpack Ready
- ☐ Put Shoes On

BEDTIME

- ☐ Clean Room
- ☐ Bath Time
- ☐ Put On Pajamas
- ☐ Brush Teeth
- ☐ Potty Time
- ☐ Read Book
- ☐ Goodnight Kiss

Today Is:_______________

MORNING

- ☐ Make Your Bed
- ☐ Get Dressed
- ☐ Eat Breakfast
- ☐ Brush Teeth
- ☐ Brush Hair
- ☐ Get Backpack Ready
- ☐ Put Shoes On

BEDTIME

- ☐ Clean Room
- ☐ Bath Time
- ☐ Put On Pajamas
- ☐ Brush Teeth
- ☐ Potty Time
- ☐ Read Book
- ☐ Goodnight Kiss

Today Is:_____________

MORNING

- ☐ Make Your Bed
- ☐ Get Dressed
- ☐ Eat Breakfast
- ☐ Brush Teeth
- ☐ Brush Hair
- ☐ Get Backpack Ready
- ☐ Put Shoes On

BEDTIME

- ☐ Clean Room
- ☐ Bath Time
- ☐ Put On Pajamas
- ☐ Brush Teeth
- ☐ Potty Time
- ☐ Read Book
- ☐ Goodnight Kiss

MORNING

- ☐ Make Your Bed
- ☐ Get Dressed
- ☐ Eat Breakfast
- ☐ Brush Teeth
- ☐ Brush Hair
- ☐ Get Backpack Ready
- ☐ Put Shoes On

BEDTIME

- ☐ Clean Room
- ☐ Bath Time
- ☐ Put On Pajamas
- ☐ Brush Teeth
- ☐ Potty Time
- ☐ Read Book
- ☐ Goodnight Kiss

Today Is:_______________

MORNING

- [ ] Make Your Bed
- [ ] Get Dressed
- [ ] Eat Breakfast
- [ ] Brush Teeth
- [ ] Brush Hair
- [ ] Get Backpack Ready
- [ ] Put Shoes On

BEDTIME

- [ ] Clean Room
- [ ] Bath Time
- [ ] Put On Pajamas
- [ ] Brush Teeth
- [ ] Potty Time
- [ ] Read Book
- [ ] Goodnight Kiss

Today Is:______________

MORNING

- ☐ Make Your Bed
- ☐ Get Dressed
- ☐ Eat Breakfast
- ☐ Brush Teeth
- ☐ Brush Hair
- ☐ Get Backpack Ready
- ☐ Put Shoes On

BEDTIME

- ☐ Clean Room
- ☐ Bath Time
- ☐ Put On Pajamas
- ☐ Brush Teeth
- ☐ Potty Time
- ☐ Read Book
- ☐ Goodnight Kiss

Today Is:____________________

MORNING

- ☐ Make Your Bed
- ☐ Get Dressed
- ☐ Eat Breakfast
- ☐ Brush Teeth
- ☐ Brush Hair
- ☐ Get Backpack Ready
- ☐ Put Shoes On

BEDTIME

- ☐ Clean Room
- ☐ Bath Time
- ☐ Put On Pajamas
- ☐ Brush Teeth
- ☐ Potty Time
- ☐ Read Book
- ☐ Goodnight Kiss

Today Is:______________

MORNING

- ☐ Make Your Bed
- ☐ Get Dressed
- ☐ Eat Breakfast
- ☐ Brush Teeth
- ☐ Brush Hair
- ☐ Get Backpack Ready
- ☐ Put Shoes On

BEDTIME

- ☐ Clean Room
- ☐ Bath Time
- ☐ Put On Pajamas
- ☐ Brush Teeth
- ☐ Potty Time
- ☐ Read Book
- ☐ Goodnight Kiss

Today Is:________________

MORNING

- [ ] Make Your Bed
- [ ] Get Dressed
- [ ] Eat Breakfast
- [ ] Brush Teeth
- [ ] Brush Hair
- [ ] Get Backpack Ready
- [ ] Put Shoes On

BEDTIME

- [ ] Clean Room
- [ ] Bath Time
- [ ] Put On Pajamas
- [ ] Brush Teeth
- [ ] Potty Time
- [ ] Read Book
- [ ] Goodnight Kiss

MORNING

- ☐ Make Your Bed
- ☐ Get Dressed
- ☐ Eat Breakfast
- ☐ Brush Teeth
- ☐ Brush Hair
- ☐ Get Backpack Ready
- ☐ Put Shoes On

BEDTIME

- ☐ Clean Room
- ☐ Bath Time
- ☐ Put On Pajamas
- ☐ Brush Teeth
- ☐ Potty Time
- ☐ Read Book
- ☐ Goodnight Kiss

Today Is:______________

MORNING

- ☐ Make Your Bed
- ☐ Get Dressed
- ☐ Eat Breakfast
- ☐ Brush Teeth
- ☐ Brush Hair
- ☐ Get Backpack Ready
- ☐ Put Shoes On

BEDTIME

- ☐ Clean Room
- ☐ Bath Time
- ☐ Put On Pajamas
- ☐ Brush Teeth
- ☐ Potty Time
- ☐ Read Book
- ☐ Goodnight Kiss

MORNING

- ☐ Make Your Bed
- ☐ Get Dressed
- ☐ Eat Breakfast
- ☐ Brush Teeth
- ☐ Brush Hair
- ☐ Get Backpack Ready
- ☐ Put Shoes On

BEDTIME

- ☐ Clean Room
- ☐ Bath Time
- ☐ Put On Pajamas
- ☐ Brush Teeth
- ☐ Potty Time
- ☐ Read Book
- ☐ Goodnight Kiss

Today Is:__________________

MORNING

- ☐ Make Your Bed
- ☐ Get Dressed
- ☐ Eat Breakfast
- ☐ Brush Teeth
- ☐ Brush Hair
- ☐ Get Backpack Ready
- ☐ Put Shoes On

BEDTIME

- ☐ Clean Room
- ☐ Bath Time
- ☐ Put On Pajamas
- ☐ Brush Teeth
- ☐ Potty Time
- ☐ Read Book
- ☐ Goodnight Kiss

MORNING

- ☐ Make Your Bed
- ☐ Get Dressed
- ☐ Eat Breakfast
- ☐ Brush Teeth
- ☐ Brush Hair
- ☐ Get Backpack Ready
- ☐ Put Shoes On

BEDTIME

- ☐ Clean Room
- ☐ Bath Time
- ☐ Put On Pajamas
- ☐ Brush Teeth
- ☐ Potty Time
- ☐ Read Book
- ☐ Goodnight Kiss

MORNING

- [ ] Make Your Bed
- [ ] Get Dressed
- [ ] Eat Breakfast
- [ ] Brush Teeth
- [ ] Brush Hair
- [ ] Get Backpack Ready
- [ ] Put Shoes On

BEDTIME

- [ ] Clean Room
- [ ] Bath Time
- [ ] Put On Pajamas
- [ ] Brush Teeth
- [ ] Potty Time
- [ ] Read Book
- [ ] Goodnight Kiss

Today Is:________________

MORNING

- ☐ Make Your Bed
- ☐ Get Dressed
- ☐ Eat Breakfast
- ☐ Brush Teeth
- ☐ Brush Hair
- ☐ Get Backpack Ready
- ☐ Put Shoes On

BEDTIME

- ☐ Clean Room
- ☐ Bath Time
- ☐ Put On Pajamas
- ☐ Brush Teeth
- ☐ Potty Time
- ☐ Read Book
- ☐ Goodnight Kiss

MORNING

- ☐ Make Your Bed
- ☐ Get Dressed
- ☐ Eat Breakfast
- ☐ Brush Teeth
- ☐ Brush Hair
- ☐ Get Backpack Ready
- ☐ Put Shoes On

BEDTIME

- ☐ Clean Room
- ☐ Bath Time
- ☐ Put On Pajamas
- ☐ Brush Teeth
- ☐ Potty Time
- ☐ Read Book
- ☐ Goodnight Kiss

Today Is:_______________

MORNING

- ☐ Make Your Bed
- ☐ Get Dressed
- ☐ Eat Breakfast
- ☐ Brush Teeth
- ☐ Brush Hair
- ☐ Get Backpack Ready
- ☐ Put Shoes On

BEDTIME

- ☐ Clean Room
- ☐ Bath Time
- ☐ Put On Pajamas
- ☐ Brush Teeth
- ☐ Potty Time
- ☐ Read Book
- ☐ Goodnight Kiss

Today Is:______________

MORNING

- ☐ Make Your Bed
- ☐ Get Dressed
- ☐ Eat Breakfast
- ☐ Brush Teeth
- ☐ Brush Hair
- ☐ Get Backpack Ready
- ☐ Put Shoes On

BEDTIME

- ☐ Clean Room
- ☐ Bath Time
- ☐ Put On Pajamas
- ☐ Brush Teeth
- ☐ Potty Time
- ☐ Read Book
- ☐ Goodnight Kiss

Today Is:_______________

MORNING

- ☐ Make Your Bed
- ☐ Get Dressed
- ☐ Eat Breakfast
- ☐ Brush Teeth
- ☐ Brush Hair
- ☐ Get Backpack Ready
- ☐ Put Shoes On

BEDTIME

- ☐ Clean Room
- ☐ Bath Time
- ☐ Put On Pajamas
- ☐ Brush Teeth
- ☐ Potty Time
- ☐ Read Book
- ☐ Goodnight Kiss

Today Is:_______________

MORNING

- ☐ Make Your Bed
- ☐ Get Dressed
- ☐ Eat Breakfast
- ☐ Brush Teeth
- ☐ Brush Hair
- ☐ Get Backpack Ready
- ☐ Put Shoes On

BEDTIME

- ☐ Clean Room
- ☐ Bath Time
- ☐ Put On Pajamas
- ☐ Brush Teeth
- ☐ Potty Time
- ☐ Read Book
- ☐ Goodnight Kiss

Today Is:________________

MORNING

- ☐ Make Your Bed
- ☐ Get Dressed
- ☐ Eat Breakfast
- ☐ Brush Teeth
- ☐ Brush Hair
- ☐ Get Backpack Ready
- ☐ Put Shoes On

BEDTIME

- ☐ Clean Room
- ☐ Bath Time
- ☐ Put On Pajamas
- ☐ Brush Teeth
- ☐ Potty Time
- ☐ Read Book
- ☐ Goodnight Kiss

Today Is:________________

<table>
<tr><td>

MORNING

☐ Make Your Bed

☐ Get Dressed

☐ Eat Breakfast

☐ Brush Teeth

☐ Brush Hair

☐ Get Backpack Ready

☐ Put Shoes On

</td><td>

BEDTIME

☐ Clean Room

☐ Bath Time

☐ Put On Pajamas

☐ Brush Teeth

☐ Potty Time

☐ Read Book

☐ Goodnight Kiss

</td></tr>
</table>

MORNING

- ☐ Make Your Bed
- ☐ Get Dressed
- ☐ Eat Breakfast
- ☐ Brush Teeth
- ☐ Brush Hair
- ☐ Get Backpack Ready
- ☐ Put Shoes On

BEDTIME

- ☐ Clean Room
- ☐ Bath Time
- ☐ Put On Pajamas
- ☐ Brush Teeth
- ☐ Potty Time
- ☐ Read Book
- ☐ Goodnight Kiss

MORNING

- ☐ Make Your Bed
- ☐ Get Dressed
- ☐ Eat Breakfast
- ☐ Brush Teeth
- ☐ Brush Hair
- ☐ Get Backpack Ready
- ☐ Put Shoes On

BEDTIME

- ☐ Clean Room
- ☐ Bath Time
- ☐ Put On Pajamas
- ☐ Brush Teeth
- ☐ Potty Time
- ☐ Read Book
- ☐ Goodnight Kiss

Today Is:_______________

MORNING	BEDTIME

MORNING

- ☐ Make Your Bed
- ☐ Get Dressed
- ☐ Eat Breakfast
- ☐ Brush Teeth
- ☐ Brush Hair
- ☐ Get Backpack Ready
- ☐ Put Shoes On

BEDTIME

- ☐ Clean Room
- ☐ Bath Time
- ☐ Put On Pajamas
- ☐ Brush Teeth
- ☐ Potty Time
- ☐ Read Book
- ☐ Goodnight Kiss

Today Is:________________

MORNING

- ☐ Make Your Bed
- ☐ Get Dressed
- ☐ Eat Breakfast
- ☐ Brush Teeth
- ☐ Brush Hair
- ☐ Get Backpack Ready
- ☐ Put Shoes On

BEDTIME

- ☐ Clean Room
- ☐ Bath Time
- ☐ Put On Pajamas
- ☐ Brush Teeth
- ☐ Potty Time
- ☐ Read Book
- ☐ Goodnight Kiss

MORNING

- ☐ Make Your Bed
- ☐ Get Dressed
- ☐ Eat Breakfast
- ☐ Brush Teeth
- ☐ Brush Hair
- ☐ Get Backpack Ready
- ☐ Put Shoes On

BEDTIME

- ☐ Clean Room
- ☐ Bath Time
- ☐ Put On Pajamas
- ☐ Brush Teeth
- ☐ Potty Time
- ☐ Read Book
- ☐ Goodnight Kiss

MORNING

- ☐ Make Your Bed
- ☐ Get Dressed
- ☐ Eat Breakfast
- ☐ Brush Teeth
- ☐ Brush Hair
- ☐ Get Backpack Ready
- ☐ Put Shoes On

BEDTIME

- ☐ Clean Room
- ☐ Bath Time
- ☐ Put On Pajamas
- ☐ Brush Teeth
- ☐ Potty Time
- ☐ Read Book
- ☐ Goodnight Kiss

MORNING

- ☐ Make Your Bed
- ☐ Get Dressed
- ☐ Eat Breakfast
- ☐ Brush Teeth
- ☐ Brush Hair
- ☐ Get Backpack Ready
- ☐ Put Shoes On

BEDTIME

- ☐ Clean Room
- ☐ Bath Time
- ☐ Put On Pajamas
- ☐ Brush Teeth
- ☐ Potty Time
- ☐ Read Book
- ☐ Goodnight Kiss

Today Is:_______________

MORNING

- [ ] Make Your Bed
- [ ] Get Dressed
- [ ] Eat Breakfast
- [ ] Brush Teeth
- [ ] Brush Hair
- [ ] Get Backpack Ready
- [ ] Put Shoes On

BEDTIME

- [ ] Clean Room
- [ ] Bath Time
- [ ] Put On Pajamas
- [ ] Brush Teeth
- [ ] Potty Time
- [ ] Read Book
- [ ] Goodnight Kiss

MORNING

- ☐ Make Your Bed
- ☐ Get Dressed
- ☐ Eat Breakfast
- ☐ Brush Teeth
- ☐ Brush Hair
- ☐ Get Backpack Ready
- ☐ Put Shoes On

BEDTIME

- ☐ Clean Room
- ☐ Bath Time
- ☐ Put On Pajamas
- ☐ Brush Teeth
- ☐ Potty Time
- ☐ Read Book
- ☐ Goodnight Kiss

MORNING

- ☐ Make Your Bed
- ☐ Get Dressed
- ☐ Eat Breakfast
- ☐ Brush Teeth
- ☐ Brush Hair
- ☐ Get Backpack Ready
- ☐ Put Shoes On

BEDTIME

- ☐ Clean Room
- ☐ Bath Time
- ☐ Put On Pajamas
- ☐ Brush Teeth
- ☐ Potty Time
- ☐ Read Book
- ☐ Goodnight Kiss

Today Is:______________

MORNING

- ☐ Make Your Bed
- ☐ Get Dressed
- ☐ Eat Breakfast
- ☐ Brush Teeth
- ☐ Brush Hair
- ☐ Get Backpack Ready
- ☐ Put Shoes On

BEDTIME

- ☐ Clean Room
- ☐ Bath Time
- ☐ Put On Pajamas
- ☐ Brush Teeth
- ☐ Potty Time
- ☐ Read Book
- ☐ Goodnight Kiss

Today Is:______________

MORNING

- ☐ Make Your Bed
- ☐ Get Dressed
- ☐ Eat Breakfast
- ☐ Brush Teeth
- ☐ Brush Hair
- ☐ Get Backpack Ready
- ☐ Put Shoes On

BEDTIME

- ☐ Clean Room
- ☐ Bath Time
- ☐ Put On Pajamas
- ☐ Brush Teeth
- ☐ Potty Time
- ☐ Read Book
- ☐ Goodnight Kiss

MORNING

- ☐ Make Your Bed
- ☐ Get Dressed
- ☐ Eat Breakfast
- ☐ Brush Teeth
- ☐ Brush Hair
- ☐ Get Backpack Ready
- ☐ Put Shoes On

BEDTIME

- ☐ Clean Room
- ☐ Bath Time
- ☐ Put On Pajamas
- ☐ Brush Teeth
- ☐ Potty Time
- ☐ Read Book
- ☐ Goodnight Kiss

Today Is:______________________

MORNING

- ☐ Make Your Bed
- ☐ Get Dressed
- ☐ Eat Breakfast
- ☐ Brush Teeth
- ☐ Brush Hair
- ☐ Get Backpack Ready
- ☐ Put Shoes On

BEDTIME

- ☐ Clean Room
- ☐ Bath Time
- ☐ Put On Pajamas
- ☐ Brush Teeth
- ☐ Potty Time
- ☐ Read Book
- ☐ Goodnight Kiss

Today Is:_______________

MORNING

- ☐ Make Your Bed
- ☐ Get Dressed
- ☐ Eat Breakfast
- ☐ Brush Teeth
- ☐ Brush Hair
- ☐ Get Backpack Ready
- ☐ Put Shoes On

BEDTIME

- ☐ Clean Room
- ☐ Bath Time
- ☐ Put On Pajamas
- ☐ Brush Teeth
- ☐ Potty Time
- ☐ Read Book
- ☐ Goodnight Kiss

MORNING

- ☐ Make Your Bed
- ☐ Get Dressed
- ☐ Eat Breakfast
- ☐ Brush Teeth
- ☐ Brush Hair
- ☐ Get Backpack Ready
- ☐ Put Shoes On

BEDTIME

- ☐ Clean Room
- ☐ Bath Time
- ☐ Put On Pajamas
- ☐ Brush Teeth
- ☐ Potty Time
- ☐ Read Book
- ☐ Goodnight Kiss

MORNING

- ☐ Make Your Bed
- ☐ Get Dressed
- ☐ Eat Breakfast
- ☐ Brush Teeth
- ☐ Brush Hair
- ☐ Get Backpack Ready
- ☐ Put Shoes On

BEDTIME

- ☐ Clean Room
- ☐ Bath Time
- ☐ Put On Pajamas
- ☐ Brush Teeth
- ☐ Potty Time
- ☐ Read Book
- ☐ Goodnight Kiss

Today Is:_______________

MORNING

- ☐ Make Your Bed
- ☐ Get Dressed
- ☐ Eat Breakfast
- ☐ Brush Teeth
- ☐ Brush Hair
- ☐ Get Backpack Ready
- ☐ Put Shoes On

BEDTIME

- ☐ Clean Room
- ☐ Bath Time
- ☐ Put On Pajamas
- ☐ Brush Teeth
- ☐ Potty Time
- ☐ Read Book
- ☐ Goodnight Kiss

Today Is:_______________

MORNING

- ☐ Make Your Bed
- ☐ Get Dressed
- ☐ Eat Breakfast
- ☐ Brush Teeth
- ☐ Brush Hair
- ☐ Get Backpack Ready
- ☐ Put Shoes On

BEDTIME

- ☐ Clean Room
- ☐ Bath Time
- ☐ Put On Pajamas
- ☐ Brush Teeth
- ☐ Potty Time
- ☐ Read Book
- ☐ Goodnight Kiss

Today Is:________________

MORNING

- ☐ Make Your Bed
- ☐ Get Dressed
- ☐ Eat Breakfast
- ☐ Brush Teeth
- ☐ Brush Hair
- ☐ Get Backpack Ready
- ☐ Put Shoes On

BEDTIME

- ☐ Clean Room
- ☐ Bath Time
- ☐ Put On Pajamas
- ☐ Brush Teeth
- ☐ Potty Time
- ☐ Read Book
- ☐ Goodnight Kiss

Today Is:________________

MORNING

- ☐ Make Your Bed
- ☐ Get Dressed
- ☐ Eat Breakfast
- ☐ Brush Teeth
- ☐ Brush Hair
- ☐ Get Backpack Ready
- ☐ Put Shoes On

BEDTIME

- ☐ Clean Room
- ☐ Bath Time
- ☐ Put On Pajamas
- ☐ Brush Teeth
- ☐ Potty Time
- ☐ Read Book
- ☐ Goodnight Kiss

www.ingramcontent.com/pod-product-compliance
Lightning Source LLC
Chambersburg PA
CBHW081928120726
47997CB00010B/3082